# EMOJIS

## THE SECRET BEHIND THE SMILE

MARTY ALLEN



DOG 'n' BONE

PUBLISHED IN 2015 BY DOG 'N' BONE BOOKS
AN IMPRINT OF RYLAND PETERS & SMALL LTD
20–21 JOCKEY'S FIELDS
LONDON WC1R 4BW

341 E 116TH ST
NEW YORK, NY 10029

WWW.RYLANDPETERS.COM

10 9 8 7 6 5 4 3 2



A CIP catalog record for this book is available from the Library of Congress and the British Library.

ISBN: 978 1 909313 73 6

Printed in China

Designer: Eoghan O'Brien
Additional Emoji illustrations on pages 38–41 by Dan Prange

Commissioning editor: Pete Jorgensen
Art director: Sally Powell
Production controller: Sarah Kulasek-Boyd
Publishing manager: Penny Craig
Publisher: Cindy Richards

# CONTENTS

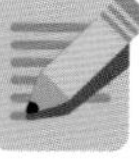

INTRODUCTION

# AN EMOJI IS BORN

# EMOJIS...

Cute and silly pictures that suddenly live inside of all of our messages and devices.

It seems like only yesterday that a string of letters combining to form a word was a sufficient method to convey information. But in our endless pursuit to abbreviate and articulate we've created a new and oddly universal language: Emojis.

Here at The Emoji Institute (you can learn more about us by visiting emoji-institute.com) we examine from all angles this phenomenon that has infiltrated our lives and languages. In this text we'll tackle their history (to date), their use, their culture, what's missing, what's coming, and more. We even get to know a select assortment of characters in some rare Emoji interviews and propose a few Emoji-based extra-curricular activities.

Buckle up, kids and cadets. Emojis are here to stay and it's time to get to know them. Or her. Or it. Or '👾'.

# WHAT IS AN EMOJI?

Emoji was born in Japan. Emoji literally translates to, "picture letter." 

This makes sense. For the uninitiated, this is an Emoji: This guy is, too:

But they aren't all delightful little creatures. These objects and symbols are also all Emojis:

Simply, Emojis are pictures that we incorporate into messages in order to convey basic meanings, or to enhance what we're already trying to say.

In terms of use on a computer, they are effectively their own font (or typeface). Like any font, they are broken into groupings of "characters," but with Emoji, this idea is given a whole new meaning, as each character is much more than a single letter. Where a standard font is made up of an alphabet that represents phonetic sounds, the Emoji font is a series of open-ended pictures and symbols. Their meanings are evolving and can change with each user's interpretation.

At the time of writing, there are currently 722 Emojis, with plans for many more arriving soon. Typically, they are roughly organized in the following categories: faces, objects, animals, seasons, flags, symbols, etc.

Emojis are available to be viewed in almost all of our electronic devices, big and small, most often used in text messages, e-mail, social media, and web pages. Due to international standardization, the nature of the symbols has been made uniform, though their appearance changes slightly based on the platform they are viewed on (more on that later).

The sum total is that, regardless of whether you find them to be adorable and useful or hideous and obtrusive, they're pretty much everywhere.

# WHY USE EMOJIS? Now we're getting personal. 

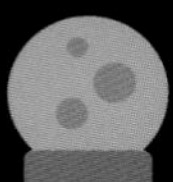

## WHY USE EMOJIS INSTEAD OF WORDS AND LETTERS?

While some here at The Emoji Institute suspect a conspiracy involving the pyramids and space aliens...

...most would argue that they enhance the conversation. Others say they lighten the mood. Some might suggest they add emphasis or clarify intent.

For our youngest demographics, it's considered abnormal NOT to see an Emoji attached to a message.

As in: Hey how r u? No Emoji? What's wrong?

## WHY HAVE THEY TAKEN OVER NOW?

Countless theories persist, but in light of our increased reliance upon typing two-fingered messages on tiny devices it seems logical that a simple digital pictographic system would catch on.

Perhaps amidst our exponential reliance upon digital communications we miss the nuance of what a real face can convey, and little pictures of shoes and eggplants are a way to compensate?

Maybe the answer is as simple as they come:

They're easy to use, they're fun, and they're funny.

While one could argue that Emojis are the next logical step in a culture obsessed with increasingly depersonalized communication, it wouldn't matter. Because they are here, and every person under the age of 20 is using them, and your Mom probably is too. Get with it.

EMOJI EXTRA CURRICULAR 1:

# WHICH EMOJI ARE YOU?

Here at the Emoji Institute we've devised an iron-clad system for determining your inner Emoji. Answer the following five questions and reveal your soul to the world.

**1. What is your favorite holiday?**

A. Christmas
B. Halloween
C. I hate holidays
D. Valentine's Day
E. New Year's Eve
F. I make my own holidays

**2. What is your ideal meal?**

A. Sunny side up eggs and juice
B. Cheeseburger and a stiff drink
C. It all makes me fat
D. A shared plate of pasta
E. Sushi
F. Making something from whatever I can find...

**3. What is your idea of a perfect day off?**

A. Relaxing with good friends and family
B. Partying all day and night
C. I never get days off!
D. Spending all day with my one true love
E. Trying something new
F. Discovering an alien species and then leaving the planet with them

**4. What is your favorite color?**

A. Blue
B. Red
C. Black
D. Pink
E. Anything neon
F. All the rainbows

**5. What is your perfect holiday destination?**

A. Disneyworld
B. The bar
C. I don't get vacations, either!
D. Paris
E. Australia
F. Mars

Tally the total number of each letter you've answered. The letter you have the most of is your DOMINANT Emoji trait. If you have chosen any other letter answer at least twice, you have Shared Emoji Syndrome (SES), with other tendencies toward that Emoji–don't be alarmed, this is very common. And if you are the rare creature with no dominant choice and ties all over the place then you are an Emoji Lord, please contact the Emoji Institute immediately.

# IF YOU ARE:

**A dominant:** You are Smiling Face Emoji! Mr. or Mrs. Happiness. You love life and living it! Aren't you just delightful!?!

**B dominant:** You are Smiling Face with Horns Emoji! The Little Devil. You like the wicked side of life, and you don't care who knows it!

**C dominant:** You are Mad Emoji! The Grump. And that's ok with us, just don't yell.

**D dominant:** You are Smiling Cat with Heart Eyes Emoji! The lover. A regular cupid wrapped in a Romeo and smothered in a Juliet. You can't get enough matters of the heart to satisfy you!

**E dominant:** You are Dancer Emoji! The Adventurer. No challenge goes unanswered in your wild world. You don't wait to hear the call of adventure, you're already out the door.

**F dominant:** You are Alien Monster Emoji! The Weird One. You dance to your own song as played on imaginary instruments. Is it strange? Not only do you not care, you prefer it that way.

CHAPTER 1

# THE HISTORY OF EMOJIS

# ANCIENT ROOTS

Communicating with one another via pictures isn't a new idea. Our earliest attempts were paintings on cave walls from as many as 40,000 years ago. Who knew cave men were so close to being able to send text messages?

Cave paintings are an example of a pictogram, or using a symbol to represent an object. Does this sound familiar?

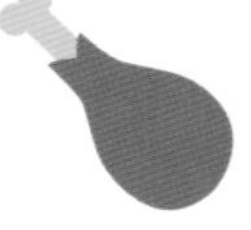

We again see pictograms creep into ancient written languages as they fuse with the close cousin of the pictogram, the good old ideogram. An ideogram takes the system a bit further and uses pictures to represent an idea.

The Sumerians then made some pictographic strides with cuneiform, using shapes such as triangles and stars to represent sounds.

Picture-based language really took off when the Egyptians got their hands on hieroglyphics, a complex system of pictograms and ideograms.

They talked about cats a lot, too.

Many other examples of our proud pictographic lineage exist throughout the history of written language, notably in the roots of Chinese, Korean, and Japanese language.

Say, aren't Emojis from Japan?

# MODERN RELATIVES

Sure, pictures have been creeping in and out of our written language since we were grunting about fire. But how did we get from a bison on a cave wall to this guy to the right? There's a meandering little path that leads from our more modern-day pictographic cousins to the Emojis we know and love today.

The most dominant form of international pictograms which we know and rely upon are those of public signs.

From when to walk to where to change the baby, street signs are a direct predecessor to our everyday Emojis. How else would you know which restroom is yours, where to swim, and when to yield?

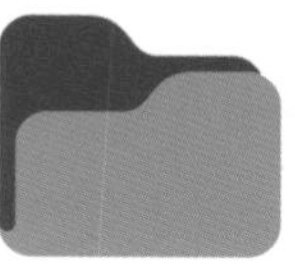

Pictographic symbols are common. They're in comic books, instruction manuals, and on your computer screen. That isn't a REAL file cabinet inside your laptop.

Or is it!?!

All of these examples bridge the gap of a lack of a common tongue in favor of pictures conveying ideas.

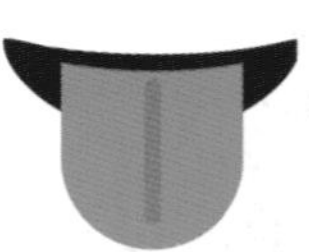

# EMOTICONS

No discussions about the history of the pictorial text language family would be complete without mentioning the closest cousins of all in the evolution of Emojis: the emoticon. Short for "emotional icons," these guys have been around for a surprisingly long time, with early stabs at the form as far back as 1850s' telegrams.

However, the modern iconic emoticon and its subsequent widespread use is largely attributed to computer programmer Scott Fahlman, who in 1982 officially proposed the now iconic characters below:

:-) and :-(

This pair were designed to be read as "happy" and "sad," respectively. Scott Fahlman hit the brief with aplomb, earning him legend status here at the Emoji Institute. The distinguishing features of emoticons are that the reader must turn his or head sideways to read them and that they are made up of symbols already held within a given font set. These basic character combinations have gone far since then, providing inspiration for the creation of numerous popular Emojis.

Where Emoji makes history is in creating it's own standardized font set to express our inner smileys... but how did these little pictures pull off their worldwide acclaim?

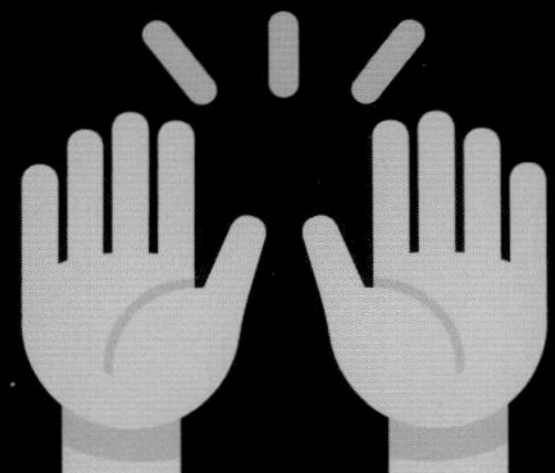

# EMOJI AND MR. KURITA

In the late 1990's a man named Shigetaka Kurita worked for a Japanese company called NTT-Docomo, specializing in the then-fledgling industry of mobile internet development. His company had found success introducing a heart symbol to its pagers a few years before. They were looking for their next big thing.

Mr. Kurita noticed a problem with modern Japanese digital communication. The normally verbose and formalized language was losing nuance when transposed into the form of e-mail and other plugged-in interactions. This often caused confusion and misplaced hurt feelings. He thought that if he could come up with simple symbols like Docomo's successful heart to add to text he could address the problem of adding the necessary emotional clarity to online messaging.

He set about creating 176 12-pixel by 12-pixel characters that represented the entirety of human emotion. And he didn't know how to draw.

The results were decidedly more primitive-looking than our contemporary Emojis, but the foundation had been laid.

Various efforts at creating a uniform standard were set upon with varying degrees of success. While the jury is still out on how well the standardization process has ever worked, the most significant step toward it, which also led to Emojis' international fame, and use was its adoption into Unicode Standard...

# WHAT THE HECK IS A UNICODE? 

The Unicode Consortium is a non-profit group of programmers dedicated to creating a consistent encoding standard across all of computing. Basically, it's a bunch of benevolent nerds who make it so that our computers and phones all talk to each other in the same way.

In 2010 Emojis were added to the international Unicode Standard, paving the way for international use and your ability to really let your friends know that you crave a slice of pineapple.

   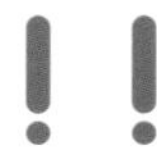

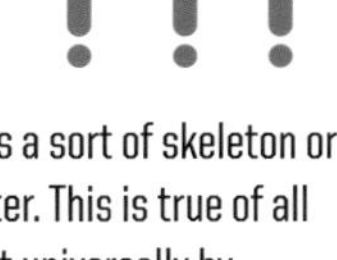

Unicode standardization acts as a sort of skeleton or guidepost for any given character. This is true of all accepted fonts and used almost universally by programmers at this point, but is particularly interesting in light of Emoji.

The result is that, while we have a standard set of 722 Emoji characters (and counting), the specific way they look can and does change depending on your given provider.

## THE EMOJI GAP

This is why your yellow heart Emoji on your iPhone looks like a weird hairy heart on your friend's Android. (You shouldn't hang out with Android people, anyways.)

Often an individual company's brand standards are applied, resulting in confusion, odd behavior, and what has become known as The Emoji Gap (a gap best filled with tiny hairy hearts).

The current popular standards for display are Unicode, Apple, Google, Twitter, and Microsoft, and they all look a little different, depending on the given Emoji. Time will tell if one uniform set of Emojis can ever truly emerge and rule the planet. Best to just remember to be careful with your tiny colored hearts and know that when in doubt, try using actual words instead.

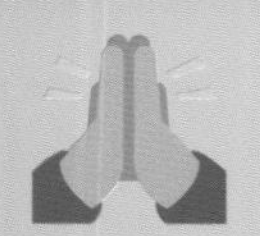

## CHAPTER 2

# PROPER USE OF EMOJIS

## EMOJI GRAMMAR 101

The mere mention of applying a grammatical standard to something like Emojis is admittedly a little nonsensical. They are weird pictures. They do what they want. Nonetheless, a few informal patterns of communication have emerged (all of which will have inevitably changed before this text was ever printed). Dare we call them grammar? Probably not...

# PLACEMENT

Go ahead, put your Emojis wherever you'd like.

But the resounding standard that has emerged is this: Emojis placed for emphasis are positioned at the end of a statement. As in:

Hey let's go get some pizza! 

This is also true when clarifying or emphasizing the emotional tone of a pressing matter:

This day was the worst, kill me!

(Note that the gun must always point AT its target, class!)

Emojis do sometimes appear mid-tweet or text, but in general they are still used to at least complete a thought. As in:

I'm crazy tired! But it's ok, I can't wait to hang out at the jeans store and drink margaritas later!

Typically the sentiment is fully summarized, though in some circles this construction might be preferred:

I'm crazy tired! But it's ok, I can't wait to hang out at the jeans store and drink margaritas later!

This version is still considered acceptable use.

It should be noted that some people simply like to include any Emojis they like anywhere in a message, or send Emojis in order to just add a little color and fun to their communication. Those people are wrong (just kidding!).

The most pressing concern with Emoji use (and indeed much of communication) is that of considering your audience, or whomever you are communicating with. If they share your particular language of Emoji use with you, then you'll understand one another. But Nana might get confused by the appearance of several tiny expressive faces in her "Happy Birthday" text...

# EMOJI LOVE NOTES

In the end, the purest form of the Emoji is the simplest: the love note. All you need is ♥...or is it?

Of all the Emojis, those expressing love and various other shades of amorous intent are some of the most abundant.

The big question is: what works best?

Start demure? Choose a simple bit of blush to let that special someone know you're thinking of a little more than just "Hello."

Or why not drop the wink to take it to the next level...

...or let go of all pretense of mystery and go full heart eyes, as if to say, "ALL I CAN SEE IS LOVE! LOOK AT ME LOOKING AT YOU!"

Perhaps you've already won Mister or Ms. Right over? How to keep things fresh? Add some spice to that text message with...

...a blushing little kiss...

...or double-down and drop the heart-wink to really ignite sparks...

...or bring the weird with the heart-eyed cat as if to say "ALL I CAN SEE IS LOVE! LOOK AT ME, I AM SO IN LOVE! I AM ALSO A CAT!"

And what of the vast array of heart colors at your disposal? Here, as in so many matters of the heart, you must make the final decision. Consider this your paint-box of love, perhaps a blue heart means you miss the one you love and a green heart means you covet them?

Ready for the next level? Lips and diamonds are one step away from...

  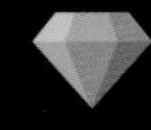

...THE LOVE HOTEL.

And if this love was not meant to be?

There's always No Lady with her unmistakable rebuff. Someday someone will win that No Lady over.

# READING IN EMOJI

In general, as on page 19, Emoji-based "sentences," or stories, progress in a Westernized left-to-right manner, like reading a very tiny book. As if to say:

"Don't look at your present under the Christmas tree!"

Otherwise this simple inversion:

...might read: "It is Christmas. I got a present for your blind monkey."

No one wants to make that mistake twice, it'll definitely ruin Christmas.

# CHAPTER 3

# MEET THE EMOJIS

## EMOJI INTERVIEWS

A lesser-known quality of all Emojis is that they have a life of their own. Here at the Emoji Institute we were lucky enough to catch up with a few Emoji luminaries to get their rarified perspectives in these unprecedented Emoji interviews.

## OFFICIAL EMOJI DESIGNATION: **SMILING FACE WITH HORNS**

## EMOJI STREET NAME: **HAPPY DEVIL**

**Emoji Institute:** So Happy Devil, what are you so happy about?

**Happy Devil:** Generally speaking, all things evil: oppressive dictatorships, social irresponsibility, unkindness toward your fellow man or animals, etc. The fun stuff.

**Emoji Institute:** Do you have any advice for aspiring evil-doers?

**Happy Devil:** Don't stay in school. Do unto others a bunch of mean stuff. And be sure to eat plenty of fiber.

## OFFICIAL EMOJI DESIGNATION: **IMP**

## STREET NAME: **SAD DEVIL**

**Emoji Institute:** Are you sad?

**Sad Devil:** Who told you that? Have you been talking to Happy Devil? I hate that guy, he keeps stealing all my thunder. And my fiber.

**Emoji Institute:** But why so sad?

**Sad Devil:** I'm a severed head with no body, no arms, no legs, nothin'! Nobody seems to care about that around here. Do you think you'd like that?!? Weary Face gets me...

## OFFICIAL EMOJI DESIGNATION: **POLICE OFFICER**

## STREET NAME: **THE COP**

**Emoji Institute:** So you're the law around here?

**The Cop:** Well, I don't like to brag, but I'm happy to keep the peace if there's another scuffle between that Sassy Ghost and the old Half Moon.

**Emoji Institute:** What's the craziest crime you've seen?

**The Cop:** I'd have to go with the time I caught pants Emoji streaking. There are some things an Emoji just can't un-see...

## OFFICIAL EMOJI DESIGNATION: **WEARY CAT FACE**

## STREET NAME: **SCREAMING KITTY**

**Emoji Institute:** What is it?! What do you see?!?

**Screaming Kitty:** The horror! The kitty-cat horror!

**Emoji Institute:** It's OK, Screaming Kitty! You can tell us! What is it?

**Screaming Kitty:** YOU! I SEE YOU! All of you out there typing us into your messages! Using us for emphasis! I can see it! And I ask you: WHAT AM I?!? WHY?!

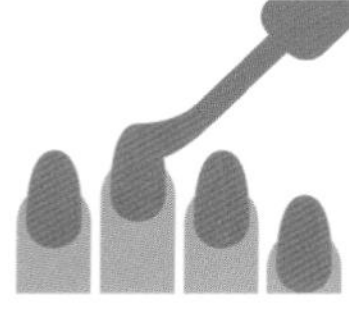

## OFFICIAL EMOJI DESIGNATION: **NAIL POLISH**
## STREET NAME: **LADY FINGERS**

**Emoji Institute:** Are you getting ready for that special someone?

**Lady Fingers:** Yeah—me, myself, and I.

**Emoji Institute:** Ah, touché. Do you always choose the same color polish?

**Lady Fingers:** Oh heck no—pink for music festivals, red for the late nights, green for good luck, and black for the poetry slam. I've got colors for all the occasions. Just don't bother me while I'm drying.

## OFFICIAL EMOJI DESIGNATION: **PILE OF POO**
## STREET NAME: **HAPPY POOP**

**Emoji Institute:** Thanks for making the time, Mr. Poop.

**Happy Poop:** It's a pleasure. And please, call me Happy.

**Emoji Institute:** Wow, great! OK Happy, I have to ask: has all the fame gone to your head?

**Happy Poop:** Every day I'm not flushed down a toilet is a gift.

**Emoji Institute:** Wow. Inspiring. Any advice for young poops out there?

**Happy Poop:** Just be the poop that you are. Don't try to cover up your smell with matches or pretend like you didn't happen at all. You're a beautiful part of nature, embrace yourself.

## OFFICIAL EMOJI DESIGNATION: **HEAVY BLACK HEART**

## STREET NAME: **HEART**

**Emoji Institute:** So Heart Emoji, what is this crazy little thing we call "love?"

**Heart:** Who's to say? A random firing of hormones and synapses, an idle twitch of the hand of fate? Does it matter at the end of the day? Some might say, "It's all that we have." I say, "Don't worry about it."

**Emoji Institute:** Any advice for folks looking for love out there?

**Heart:** Online dating is really just the worst. Cut that stuff out and go outside, already.

## OFFICIAL EMOJI DESIGNATION: **BROKEN HEART**

## STREET NAME: **AS ABOVE**

**Emoji Institute:** Do you want to talk about it?

**Broken Heart:** No! I want ice cream.

**Emoji Institute:** Hey, maybe you should get back on the horse! I can introduce you to my friend Yellow Heart Emoji?

**Broken Heart:** YELLOW HEART! ARE YOU SERIOUS? DO I LOOK THAT DESPERATE TO YOU!?!

**Emoji Institute:** Sorry, sorry, too soon—I get it.

**Broken Heart:** OK, give him my number.

## OFFICIAL EMOJI DESIGNATION: **PERSON WITH FOLDED HANDS**

## STREET NAME: **HIGH FIVE PRAY**

**Emoji Institute:** So we have to ask, which is it: a high five or a prayer?

**High Five Pray:** Can't it be both?

**Emoji Institute:** I'm going to have to say "no" here. We need an answer on this one, the people demand it.

**High Five Pray:** Fine, it's neither if you must know. I actually mean "please" and "thank you." Though personally I prefer the open-ended interpretation.

**Emoji Institute:** Fair enough. Want to high five over it?

**High Five Pray:** I do!

## OFFICIAL EMOJI DESIGNATION: **DANCER**

## STREET NAME: **DANCIN' LADY**

**Emoji Institute:** What dance are you doing?

**Dancin' Lady:** The dance I must do changes like the wind! I am as the tides and the moon, or a stranger's sweet glance in the night: ever changing!

**Emoji Institute:** So you're every dance, all the time?

**Dancin' Lady:** Yes, except that horrible, horrible Macarena. That is no dance!

## OFFICIAL EMOJI DESIGNATION: **OCTOPUS**
## STREET NAME: **THE SQUID**

**Emoji Institute:** Are you missing a few tentacles?

**The Squid:** That's a rather personal question. And no, they're off-screen, you just can't see them.

**Emoji Institute:** When's the last time you wrapped yourself around a giant ship and pulled it to the darkest depths of the ocean?

**The Squid:** You know, not all giant squids are out to sink innocent ships and eat delicious pirates! And it's been over three days, thanks for asking!

## OFFICIAL EMOJI DESIGNATION: **BABY ANGEL**
## STREET NAME: **LIL' ANGEL**

**Emoji Institute:** Any messages from heaven?

**Lil' Angel:** Hang in there, humanity; adorableness and harps are waiting for you! And God says, "Hi!"

**Emoji Institute:** We don't mean to be indiscreet, but how did you pass away, Lil' Angel?

**Lil' Angel:** Knife fight.

## OFFICIAL EMOJI DESIGNATION: **VOLCANO**
## STREET NAME: **MR. BOOM BOOM**

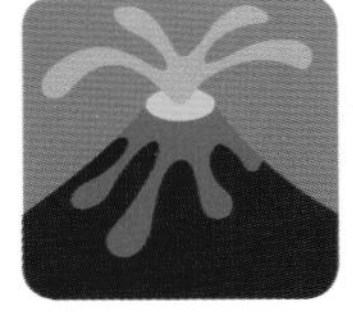

**Emoji Institute:** How often do you erupt?

**Mr. Boom Boom:** Oh, constantly. There's lava pretty much everywhere, it ruined my new rug.

**Emoji Institute:** Any regrets?

**Mr. Boom Boom:** Life moves pretty fast. One day you're a proud mountain, the next day you're destroying a village. I wish I had taken the time to really appreciate the dormancy, you know? So it goes.

## OFFICIAL EMOJI DESIGNATION: **GHOST**
## STREET NAME: **SASSY GHOST**

**Emoji Institute:** Should we be afraid of you or delighted by you?

**Sassy Ghost:** I was aiming for fear, but I'll take what I can get.

**Emoji Institute:** Any tips for terrifying new tenants?

**Sassy Ghost:** Haunting is all about the attitude. It doesn't matter if you've got designer sheets and buckets of virgin blood or just a tissue and a scab, if your heart isn't in it, they won't be scared. Go all the way or don't show up, fellow ghosts.

## OFFICIAL EMOJI DESIGNATION: BEER MUG

## STREET NAME: THE BEER

**Emoji Institute:** Beer, you're so cool. How come you're so...just...cool?

**The Beer:** I'm thinking it's simply a case of proper refrigeration.

**Emoji Institute:** HAHAHAHAHAA! You are the funniest, coolest Emoji ever. Seriously. No. Seriously! Wait...hey, I think I know that guy! Sorry, super unprofessional. Sorry. Sorry. Anyways, I have to tell you more about why I hate my Mom...

**The Beer:** Ok Emoji Institute, I think you've had enough. Let's get you into a cab.

**Emoji Institute:** No, no, I'm cool. 'Cuz my refrigerator's everywhere! Get it?!? Hey, I always wanted to tell you that your sister is cute! I love you man, you're THE GUY...Zzzzzzz...

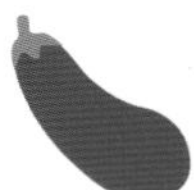

## OFFICIAL EMOJI DESIGNATION: AUBERGINE

## STREET NAME: THE EGGPLANT

**Emoji Institute:** So Eggplant, we'll cut to the chase here and get to the controversy. In an eggplant parm, do you prefer to be baked or fried?

**The Eggplant:** Baked all day. I can't stand the grease. And I'll tell you a secret: I don't mind canned sauce, either. I kind of prefer it!

**Emoji Institute:** Well that's just delightful!

**The Eggplant:** So you're not going ask about how I look like...you know?

**Emoji Institute:** A large purple vegetable used in many delicious dishes?

**The Eggplant:** Put me next to the peach and I'm rather... suggestive?

**Emoji Institute:** Uhhhh...suggestive of something that is surprisingly tasty when cubed and sautéed? An excellent source of vitamins and minerals?

**The Eggplant:** A penis! I look like a large purple penis! Come on man!

**The Emoji Institute:** Huh. I don't see it.

## OFFICIAL EMOJI DESIGNATION: SLICE OF PIZZA

## STREET NAME: THE SLICE

**Emoji Institute:** Can we get you in plain? Pepperoni gives us heartburn and our veggie friends aren't exactly thrilled with the meat option.

**The Slice:** No, sorry. I am absolute.

**Emoji Institute:** Why?

**The Slice:** Because life is unfair.

## OFFICIAL EMOJI DESIGNATION: MOYAI

## STREET NAME: EASTER ISLAND HEAD

**Emoji Institute:** So, any ancient secrets of the universe to reveal to us?

**Easter Island Head:** Sure, tons of them. What would you like to know about in particular?

**Emoji Institute:** Where do all of my lost socks go?

**Easter Island Head:** There's a lost sock vortex behind every dryer that transports socks to Sock Puppet City where they become colorful creatures who sing songs. Anything else?

**Emoji Institute:** Oh, wow. Good answer. Ok...geez. I guess, we'll go big, then. What's the secret of a happy life?

**Easter Island Head:** There's no secret at all. Happiness can be found in even the darkest of times if we remember only to turn on the lights!

**Emoji Institute:** That's so profound! Hey, wait, isn't that a Dumbledore quote?!?

**Easter Island Head:** Um, no? Fine, fine. Be...um, excellent to each other! And don't touch my stuff or I'll end you.

**Emoji Institute:** And 42?

**Easter Island Head:** And 42.

EMOJI EXTRA CURRICULAR 2:

# MAKE YOUR OWN EMOJI!

With 722 Emojis (and counting), you'd think that would be enough. But for each special snowflake of a person there's a unique Emoji, too. Here at the Emoji Institute we've devised a fool-proof method for designing your own individual character in just a few easy steps!

First choose your EMOJI HEAD SHAPE:

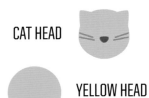

CAT HEAD

YELLOW HEAD

HUMAN HEAD ONE

HUMAN HEAD TWO

Now for the window to your Emoji soul, EMOJI EYES:

HAPPY EYES

LOVE-FILLED EYES

ANGRY EYES

SURPRISED EYES

BLUE EYES

BROWN EYES

CLOSED EYES

CARTOON EYES

CRAZY EYES

But eyes can't say it all. Tell us how you really feel with your EMOJI EXPRESSION:

HAPPY

CONFUSED

HUMAN SMILE

INDIFFERENT

KISSING

LIPSTICK

SHOCKED

TONGUE OUT

SAD

Does your character need a new EMOJI HAIRDO? Or maybe he or she is happy with just a Kojak-inspired chrome dome?

MALE HAIR

FEMALE HAIR

And what about up top with some EMOJI HEADGEAR?

SANTA HAT

TIARA

HARD HAT

SUNHAT

CAP

Finally, make your Emoji really scream "Y-O-U" with unique EMOJI FEATURES:

BEARDS

GLASSES

MUSTACHES

# PIECING IT ALL TOGETHER

Now all that is left is to scan or photocopy this page and Frankenstein your Emoji-self together using your friendly neighborhood image editing program or go old-school with some craft glue, and scissors. As has been implied several times, this is a book, not a computer, people.

Alternatively, simply copy some of the elements on the previous spread (or come up with some new ones of your own) onto the faces below. Now get to work!

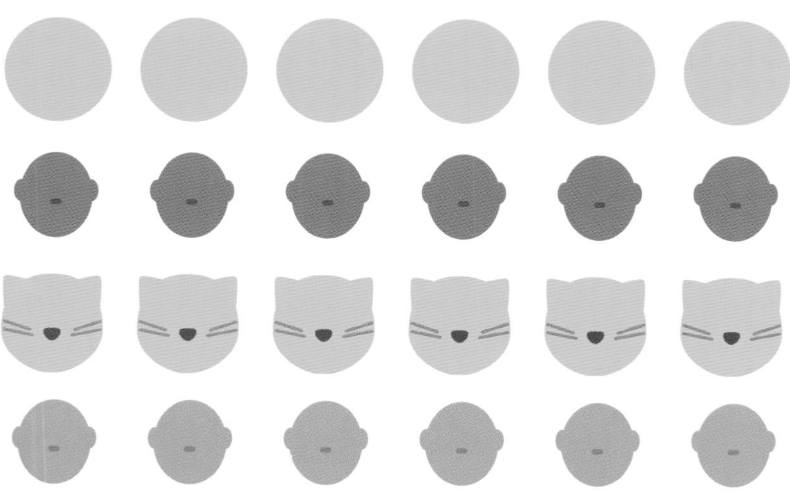

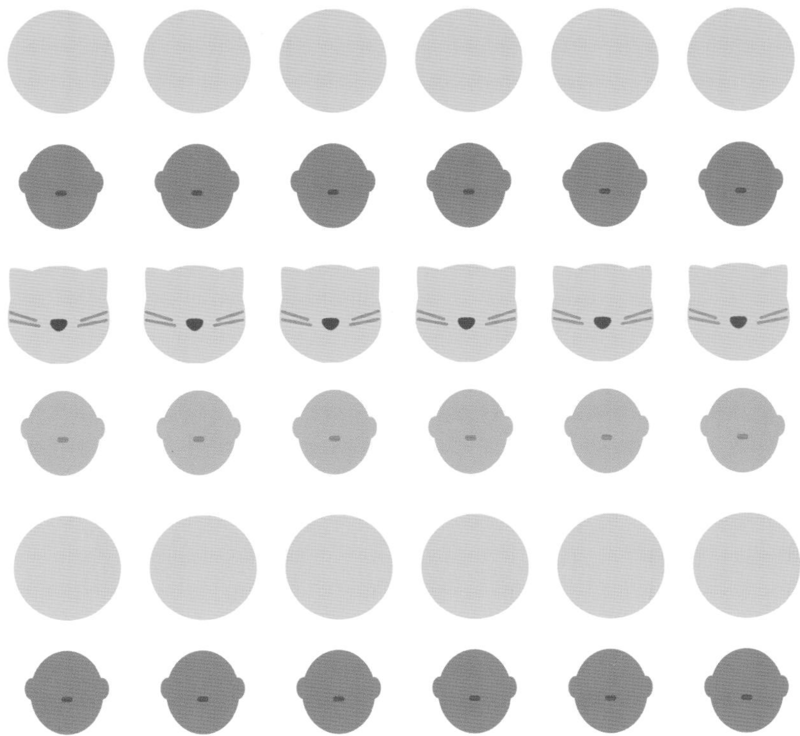

# EMOJIS WE WANT TO SEE

Unfortunately, there just aren't enough Emojis out there to cover all bases. If you're a sports nut or an animal lover you're well catered for, but what about those of us who like to do things a little differently? In the spirit of inclusivity, we've decided to put things right and create a new set of characters and creatures for those poor souls who've been overlooked. Take notes, Unicode Consortium.

**HIPSTER EMOJI** Do you remember the first time you used an Emoji? Well, the Hipster Emoji was using them way before then. He dropped his first 👍 in 2011, when Apple added the Emoji keyboard to the iPhone 📲, and has never looked back ➡➡➡. He knows how to use them properly, whether that's dripping with irony—"Who has an Americano ☕ these days? I'm all about a cold-brewed ⛄, triple-filtered Aeropress using single origin beans"—or used to discuss the oh-so-cool things he's into that us mere mortals won't yet have heard of. "This bowl of tonkotsu 🍜 really is the best in the city. The staff only speak Japanese, so you need to know your katakana, but my travels through 🗾 mean it's not a problem for me." Face it, my friend, this Emoji's way cooler than you. Deal with it 💁.

**RAPPER EMOJI** Blessed with the 🌍's biggest ego, the Rapper Emoji has a self belief only matched by his self-proclaimed genius 📢. Whether it's dropping lyrical 💣💣💣 or designing a 👕 for his latest fashion collaboration, this braggadocian beast is only too happy to tell you that he's bigger than ⛪ or that his wife has the finest 🍑 in 🇺🇸. What a load of 💩.

**FAKE TAN EMOJI** Super vain and desperate for an endless , the Fake Tan Emoji dreams of lazy days spent lounging by the , grilling herself in 100-degree protected by little more than a and the umbrella emerging from her . But when it's winter and you find yourself struggling through every morning to get to work, the natural glow fades faster than Keanu Reeves' hopes of picking up an Oscar for best actor . Thankfully, San Tancisco Beauty Salon has opened up nearby and our fake tan can spend all her hard-earned catching some UV rays. This Emoji won't be happy until she's shrivelled her skin in the quest to permanently transform her complexion into an unhealthy shade of Oompa-Loompa .

**GOTH EMOJI** It's not all in the Emoji , you know. For some, life is a lot more serious... really, really . You see, the Goth Emoji looks for something more than hanging out with , pinging their with pictures of cute s and s. It's more about the for the in the , seeing the in and . People like to tell Goth Emojis to cheer up , but they're doing just fine, thank you very much .

**BIKER EMOJI** Born to be wild ! Being a biker is so appealing when you're a young, care-free badass . 20 years later, when your days are spent working at an accountancy firm totting up the for your client's tax return, you're in danger of looking a little tragic dressed in your leathers. Thankfully the Biker Emoji doesn't give a 's ass. Soon he'll be jumping on his "hog," and hitting the road...he's just got to pick up his daughter from class first. indeed!

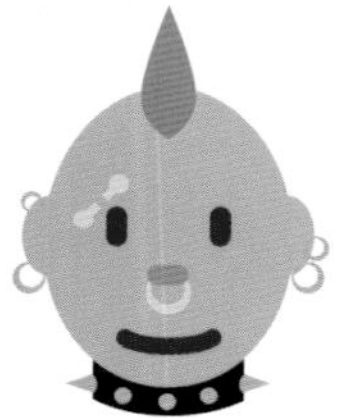

**PUNK** You need to be 💪 if you're going to fight the establishment as a Punk Emoji. First, un-🔌 and kill your 📺. Really 👊 authority in the 😐 and 🔥 that 👔. And if you want to get truly punk, you want to start a band, so you'll need to learn three 🎸 chords and take up 💉ing. Just don't lose your parents' ☎️ #️⃣ if you want to see 🍟 ever again.

**NERD** Let's face it, life as a Nerd Emoji isn't as terrible as it once was. Sure, your days are still filled with 💻s, 🔬s, and 📚s, and ⚾s just plain confuse you. Then there is 💬 with the opposite sex, which is still an intimidating storm of sorrow. But the 😎 kids are catching up, mostly because the nerds have been busy inventing 📱. So if you ever feel down about your social status, Nerd Emoji, console yourself by throwing stray 💲s from your private 🚁.

**ASTRONAUT EMOJI** Life orbiting 🌍 isn't all anti-gravity and space 🍦 for the Astronaut Emoji. Say it's a lazy Sunday and you decide to take the 🚀 for a spin to the 🌛. Unfortunately, you didn't even see that red 🚦 past Orion's Belt ⭐⭐⭐. Next thing you know you're in an interstellar 🔫 fight with a whole bunch of angry 👾👾👾. Time to 📞 the president. Again!

**MERMAID** Under the , all the are , but down there life for a Mermaid Emoji isn't all it's cracked up to be. Sure, there are singing s pretty much everywhere, but say you crave some "me time" and want to give your a mani-pedi? The means you will never get them dried. And you can forget about and . When your choices of potential mates are between a and a , you stop wondering how the whole no-legs-in-the-bedroom situation would even work, anyways. Maybe you should sell your to that lady after all? What could possibly go wrong?

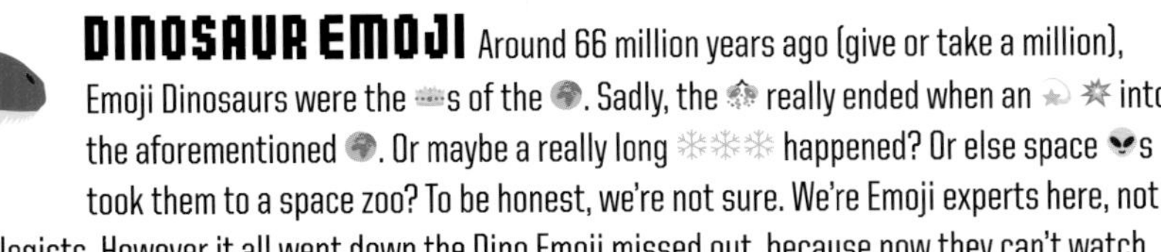

**DINOSAUR EMOJI** Around 66 million years ago (give or take a million), Emoji Dinosaurs were the s of the . Sadly, the really ended when an into the aforementioned . Or maybe a really long happened? Or else space s took them to a space zoo? To be honest, we're not sure. We're Emoji experts here, not paleontologists. However it all went down the Dino Emoji missed out, because now they can't watch , eat s, or drive around in s. And who doesn't want to see a dinosaur doing that?

**DRUG LORD EMOJI** The life of a drug lord isn't all s and s. And s and s. And lots and lots of . There are many other concerns. For instance, your personal alley isn't going to keep itself full of people throwing strikes and your international team isn't going to watch itself score goals. Not to mention the time taken up drinking plenty of high-priced bottles of with your pet named Chet. Is the constant threat of the or really worth it? Ask Chet.

# EMOJIS FOR ALL!

After a long time sitting on the core 722 Emojis, in 2015 the Unicode Consortium finally pulled it together and announced the release of 300 new characters. In addition to critically urgent newcomers like "The Middle Finger 🖕," "Man In Business Suit Levitating," and "Chipmunk," the real news is that the latest Emojis have been designed to address the much-requested need for racial diversity in Emoji Land.

These new diversified Emojis come in six skin tones based on dermatologist Thomas Fitpatrick's 1975 classification system. Below is an artist's impression of how they might look. While some pundits are still a little unhappy with the variance and believe that there is a ways to go, it's inarguable that this is at least a step forward in a more encompassing sense of Emoji equality. We here at the Emoji Institute support it wholeheartedly.

# ONE MORE EMOJI? THE HOT DOG PETITION

There is one more Emoji that didn't make the grade, but it isn't for lack of trying: the Emoji Hot Dog.

In 2014, a hot dog entrepreneur, Laura Ustick, general manager of Superdawg in Chicago, Illinois, asked the internet to get behind her in support of the Emoji Hot Dog. She started a petition, a coalition, a trending hash tag (#hotdogemoji), and was even on the national news for her efforts. Unfortunately her petition was aimed at the President of the United States and the creator of Emojis, Shigetaka Kurita. And while we love Mr. Kurita (and the Prez) as much as the next Institute, she probably should have read our book, because you won't get anywhere without addressing the Unicode Consortium. Maybe next time, hot dog lovers.

EMOJI EXTRA CURRICULAR 3:

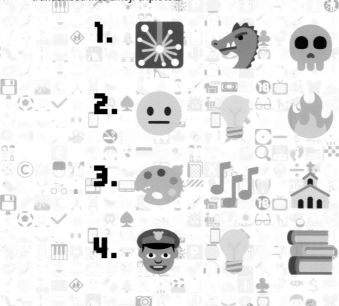

# EMOJI HISTORY PICTO-QUIZ

See if you can decode these major historical events and discoveries when deftly transcribed into Emoji triplets...

1.

2.

3.

4.

**ANSWERS:** 1. Asteroid destroys dinosaurs 2. Humans discover fire 3. The Renaissance 4. Guttenberg invents the printing press 5. The American Revolution 6. Edison invents the light bulb 7. Darwin' s Theory of Evolution 8. World War 2 9. Humans go to the moon 10. Kurita invents Emoji

## CHAPTER 4

# EMOJI CULTURE

While still a young form of expression, Emojis have already invaded countless corners of our ever-shifting cultural landscape. The Emoji Institute is dedicated to chasing any and all cultural leads. What follows is a mere sampling of the impact Emojis have had. Are you an Emoji aficionado, artisan, or auteur? Let us know, and keep the Emoji Institute up to date on all that's trending!

# EMOJI TRACKER

One of the most fascinating Emoji experiments is the Emoji tracker found at none other than emojitracker.com.

Created by artist and technology developer Matthew Rothenberg (mroth) in July of 2013, the Emoji tracker follows real-time use of Emojis on Twitter. Mr. Rothenberg even created a real-time interactive Emoji tracker at the the Eyebeam Art and Technology Center in January of 2014, encouraging visitors to interact with the tracker and influence its destiny.

At emojitracker.com you can see what's being used the most and least, and how they're being deployed. Each use on Twitter lights up the given Emoji on the website and updates the running tally. Click on any Emoji on the site and you get a real-time look at that character's usage via a live feed of tweets showing them in position.

Since its launch, emojitracker.com has analyzed a staggering 6.5 billion (that's a "B") tweets. A quick online check at the Emoji Institute shows that currently has a controversial lead over the simple . The prevalence of both can't help but lead to uncommonly optimistic conclusions about the state of our culture.

Sadly, the Baggage Claim/Customs Emojis have long made up the bottom three spots. It seems picking up your bags at the airport, walking through the "Nothing to Declare" exit, and tweeting about it just isn't as popular as it once was.

Emoji Institute Pro-tip: Type the word "disco" while checking in on the wonderful Emoji tracker for a danceable treat...

**At the time of writing, here's the list of the top ten Emojis on emojitracker.com:**

1.  2.  3.  4.   5.  6.  7.  8.  9.  10. 

# EMOJI DICK

Another truly stupefying feat of logic-defying Emoji skills is the translation of Herman Melville's "Moby Dick" into Emoji, aptly titled "Emoji Dick." The translation was edited and compiled by Fred Benenson, but was not a one-man affair. Each of the book's 10,000 sentences was translated via an elaborate crowd-sourcing system created by Amazon to farm out tiny tasks for tiny increments of money. Each sentence was translated by crowd-sourced workers three times and then voted upon by another set of workers. The funds for all of which were crowd-funded on Kickstarter. Which is quite a few crowds, all things considered.

The sum total is, of all things, an actual physical book that you can buy. Who makes those anymore? For the literature and Emoji enthusiast who has everything: "EMOJI DICK."

# GUESS THE EMOJI BOOK TITLE

"Emoji Dick" was only the beginning. Here at the Emoji Institute we've taken a long hard look at several classics of literature and re-interpreted their titles with our patented Emoji Goggles of Re-interpretation. Can you guess them all and assure your entrance into the lauded halls of the Emoji Institute? Greatness awaits.

2.

**ANSWERS:** 1. The Old Man and the Sea 2. To Kill A Mockingbird 3. A Tale of Two Cities 4. Infinite Jest 5. A Clockwork Orange 6. Crime and Punishment 7. The Grapes of Wrath 8. Animal Farm 9. Of Mice and Men 10. The Scarlet Letter 11. The Hitchhiker's Guide to the Galaxy 12. Les Misérables

# AN EMOJI ARTIST INTERVIEW: LEE MASTERSON

Emoji arts aren't all data-tracking discos and re-interpreted classics. Many traditional painters and sculptors are coming up with incorporations, representations, and twists on this young pictographic form.

The Emoji Institute was lucky enough to catch up with Brooklyn-based Emoji artist Lee Masterson for an interview. Mr. Masterson engages in printed studies of Emojis blown up to much larger scales, ultimately on either canvas or ceramic surfaces.

## What kind of Emoji art do you do?

I study Emojis by lifting the small icons seen on my phone screen and blowing them up to monumental scales. It's like looking at a flower under a microscope. Even though you can see the flower with your own eyes, when you zoom into it you find a whole new world. Typically, I make specific groupings of these Emoji to convey a narrative or social idea.

## What made you want to incorporate Emojis into your work?

We live in an extremely fun and exciting point in history and I am a sucker for any technology-based language. I always say that I may not speak other languages very well but I speak technology fluently.

## Are there any Emojis you wish you could see?

If I could see ANY Emoji for myself I guess it would be a unicorn. I am having a hard time communicating correctly with so few unicorns in my vernacular.

## What are your favorite Emoji subjects?

My favorite Emoji items are the drugs and weapons, as well as the animals! There are some dangerous dragons on my phone that are very into syringes, guns, and cocktails.

Titled: Untitled (Pill)
Materials: Porcelain and glaze with embedded pigments
Dimensions: 24 x 30 in. (60 x 76 cm)
Date: 2014

See more of Mr. Masterson's Emoji art and other conceptual works at www.leemasterson.com

# GUESS THE EMOJI TV SHOW

Here's a selection of some popular TV shows from recent years with the titles rendered expertly in Emoji. See if you are able to work out all 15. If not, you can find the answers at the bottom of the page opposite.

**ANSWERS:** 1. Mad Men 2. Six Feet Under 3. Friends 4. The Good Wife 5. How I Met Your Mother 6. Brooklyn 99 7. The Walking Dead 8. Two Broke Girls 9. The Big Bang Theory 10. Dancing with the Stars 11. Breaking Bad 12. Doctor Who 13. 24 14. House of Cards 15. Friday Night Lights

# GUESS THE EMOJI MOVIE PLOT

What makes a movie great? Compelling characters? Big stars? An amazing plot? Or how well it translates into Emoji? I think we all know the answer here. Can you guess each of the movies these Emoji scripts are summarizing?

1. 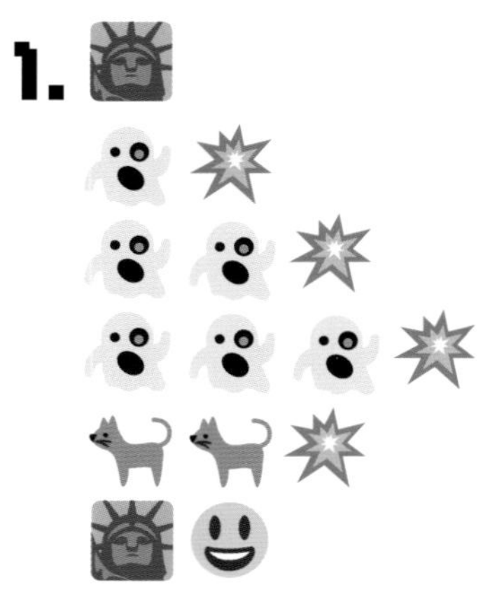

2. 

3.

4.

5.

6.

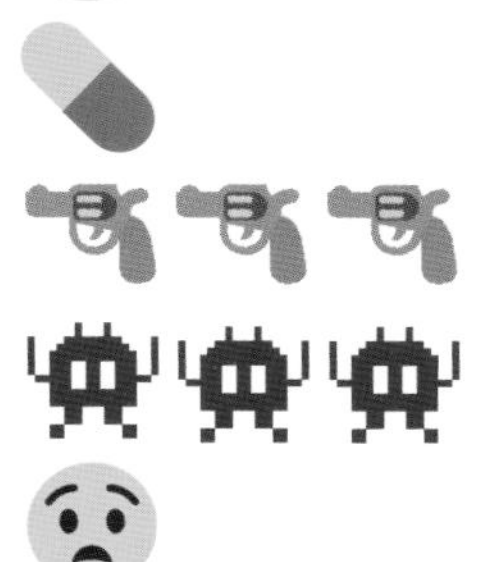

7.
8.

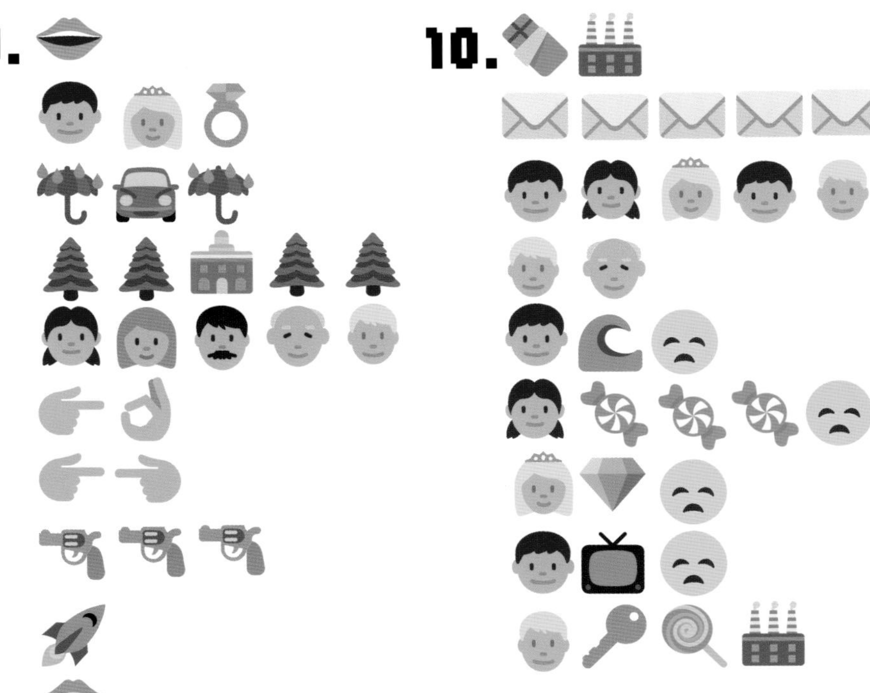


**ANSWERS:** 1. Ghostbusters 2. Stand By Me 3. The Breakfast Club 4. Donnie Darko 5. Home Alone 6. The Matrix 7. Ratatouille 8. Edward Scissorhands 9. The Rocky Horror Picture Show 10. Charlie and the Chocolate Factory

# EMOJI FUN FACTS

It is largely accepted that the original "Smiley Face" was created in 1963 by a graphic artist named Harvey Ball in Worcester, Massachusetts in order to raise morale at an insurance company that had recently fallen on hard times. It took him ten minutes to design and he was paid $45.

A big piece of why Emojis have spread so much in popularity is because in 2012 Apple included Emojis in the keyboards for its iOS 6 software. Since then Emojis' popularity has sky rocketed, and Apple's lead was followed by countless others including Facebook, Twitter, and Instagram.

A 2014 study from Match.com suggests that people who use Emojis are more likely to have sex on a regular basis!

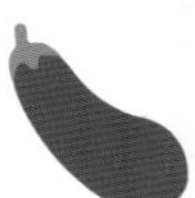

What do Canadian rapper Drake, pop star Miley Cyrus, and Atlanta Hawks basketball player Mike Scott have in common? They all have Emoji tattoos: Drake goes for , Miley chose to ink her lip with a , and Scott went crazy for Emojis and has at least 20 different characters all over his body !

Courts now consider the use of threatening Emojis like the gun and bomb as admissible evidence!

"Emoji" was added to the Oxford English Dictionary in 2013.

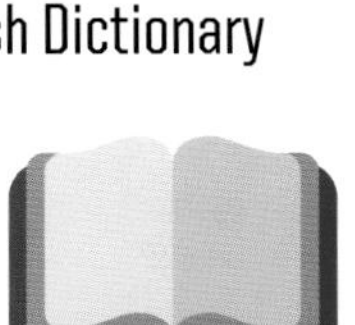

Both the Emoji creator Shigetaka Kurita and Emoticon creator Scott Fahlman think current Emoji standards are "ugly" compared to their ancestors.

# EMOJI CULTURAL EXTRAS

The contributions to Emoji culture have only just begun. Below are several more amazing experiments in Emoji. As you will hopefully find, even at this early stage of the Emoji lifespan there's enough Emoji cultural refuse for everyone's refined palate...

## THE EMOJI ART AND DESIGN SHOW

In December of 2014 an entire New York art show was dedicated to our pictographic muse. The Emoji Art and Design Show featured digital prints, sculptures, performances, and video works tackling a variety of themes by over twenty artists. Artists looked at Emojis both literally and through various cultural lenses, with primitive re-interpretations, literal tracking devices, and radical re-interpretations of classical texts.
The exhibition lives on at www.emojishow.com and shows a startling breadth of inspiration and ideas from this burgeoning medium.

## EMOJI ART HISTORY

Go further down the rabbit hole of the Emoji arts and you will find Emoji Art History. By looking up the hashtag #emojiarthistory on Twitter, you can gaze at endless representations of classic artists and artworks in Emoji form. There are a lot of them, it's kind of a thing.

Michalengelo's Creation

American Gothic

Vincent Van Gogh

...are but a few of the endless array.

# EMOJI AMONG US

How about an Emoji biopic? This delightful and beautiful short film takes a loving examination of "Emoji Among Us," using only stock footage to show Emojis active in a real-world setting. Here are a few stills from their ace video, which can be viewed here:

www.dissolve.com/showreels/emoji

# THE FUTURE OF EMOJIS

What comes next for Emojis? Who can say, but it certainly seems as though the future for our expressive little friends is very bright.

Perhaps their use will die off–another pet rock for our time. Will generations to come be staring dumb-foundedly at a poop with eyeballs and wondering once again, "What were they thinking when they came up with this?"

Or will the current trend of adding new Emojis reach a critical mass, where there are suddenly too many ways to express yourself with pictures. We at the Emoji Institute hypothesize that this could lead to the invention of MoMojis, new pictographs designed to describe our Emoji-based feelings.

Maybe our stream of pictographic friends will continue unabated until we've replaced written language entirely? A universal tongue of pictures and smiles, one globe united. A better world or a dumber place? Only our alien overlords of the future can say...

Born in the late '90s and only in prominent use since 2012, evidence seems to indicate that Emojis are here to stay. And we here at The Emoji Institute are happy to have them. Here's to our long future together, Emojis. 🎉

# EMOJI QUOTES

Like all great things, famous sayings are made even better by being translated into Emoji. Can you guess these well-known quotes and proverbs and make your grandmother proud?

**ANSWERS:** 1. To be or not to be 2. Time flies 3. Love is blind 4. A bird in the hand is worth two in the bush 5. Misery loves company 6. Where there's smoke there's fire 7. There's no time like the present

# THANKS

I confess, I was initially Emoji-reluctant and if it wasn't for the prodding of Rebecca McBride and Casey Splain I never would have opened my heart to the love of these delightful creatures. (Those ladies are also pretty good with the whole friendship, love, and support thing, too.) Hugs.

Thanks to my endless array of social media friends who spoke often and loudly about their Emoji-based feelings, your input was invaluable.

Thanks to all of the artists who generously allowed us to use their Emoji images and ideas in this work—Matthew Rothenberg, Fred Benenson, and Dissolve. You guys rock! Particular thanks to Lee Masterson for his time and awesomeness.

Special thanks to Tammy Olsen for both support and for helping me take my Emoji game to the next level.

Heart thanks to Devon Bennett for love, support, and lots of ideas for Emoji movie plots.

Endless thanks to the good people at CICO and Dog 'n' Bone Books, most notably my friend and fellow Emoji aficionado Pete Jorgensen. He knows where they keep the good stuff.

A debt of gratitude to all of The Emojis who took time out of their busy schedules to sit with me and consult on the work, with special thanks to 💩, who was a beacon of endless encouragement. I am honored to call you my friend.

And biggest of thanks to Y-O-U. I love to write words down, and that wouldn't mean a darned thing if you weren't around to read them.

# ACKNOWLEDGMENTS

It turns out the internet isn't just for naughty pictures and buying stuff, it has lots of information, too. And it's unsurprising that there is a wealth of knowledge about Emojis on the old information superhighway. This book could not have been written without the help of countless sources.

The indispensable foremost authority on all-things Emoji is undoubtedly emojipedia.org, followed closely by the strange and ubiquitous everyman's encyclopedia of our time: Wikipedia.

All of the below articles were super-helpful, you should read them. Thank you articles:
mashable.com/2014/09/03/emoji-design/
www.theverge.com/2013/3/4/3966140/how-emoji-conquered-the-world
time.com/2993508/emoji-rules-tweets/
www.vocativ.com/culture/fun/emoji-skin-tones-scale/
abcnews.go.com/blogs/lifestyle/2014/03/why-hot-dog-and-taco-emojis-probably-arent-in-your-future/
laughingsquid.com/emoji-tracker-a-website-that-lights-up-emoji-as-they-are-being-used-on-twitter/
time.com/3627738/conan-nick-offerman-wooden-emojis/
webtrends.about.com/od/Social-Media-Trends/tp/10-Amazing-Facts-about-Emoji.htm
www.youbeauty.com/relationships/study-emoji-users-have-more-sex
www.dailydot.com/crime/emoji-threat-admissible-court/

And these sites were mentioned in the text, but we'll mention them again:
http://www.emojitracker.com
http://portfolio.mroth.info
http://www.emojidick.com
http://www.emojishow.com
http://www.leemasterson.com

The images and ideas associated with "Emoji Dick" were used with the permission of Fred Benenson. All associated copyright is his.

Images from Emoji Among Us © Dissolve, Inc

The images and ideas associated with "The Emoji Tracker" were used with the permission of Matthew Rothenberg. All associated copyright is his.

The images and ideas associated with the artwork of Lee Masterson were used with the permission of the artist. All associated copyright is his.